PET CARE FOR KIDS

HAMSTERS

BY KATHRYN STEVENS

The Child's World

Published in the United States of America by The Child's World®
1980 Lookout Drive • Mankato, MN 56003-1705
800-599-READ • www.childsworld.com

Acknowledgments
The Child's World®: Mary Berendes, Publishing Director
The Design Lab: Kathleen Petelinsek, Design and Page Production

Photo Credits: 123RF.com/Stanko Mravljak: 8; Arco Images GmbH/
Alamy: 17; Cheerz/Dreamstime.com: front cover, 16 (eating); Emilia
Stasiak/Dreamstime.com: 4; Eric Isselée/Dreamstime.com: 21;
iStockphoto.com/Andres Balcazar: 9; iStockphoto.com/Emre Ogan:
5; iStockphoto.com/Geoffrey Holman: front cover, back cover (metal
wheel); iStockphoto.com/gisele: front cover, back cover, 1, 3, 20
(ball); iStockphoto.com/Juan Monino: front cover (seeds); iStockphoto.
com/Michelle Milliman: front cover, 1, 3 (castle); iStockphoto.com/Su-
san Trigg: 10; Juniors Bildarchiv/Alamy: 15; Ling Cui /Dreamstime.
com: 7; Papilio/Alamy: 11; PhotoDisc: front cover, back cover, 22, 24;
Steve Skjold/Alamy: 19; tbkmedia.de/Alamy: 13; Thomas Perkins/
Dreamstime.com: 14; Titania1980/Dreamstime.com: front cover, 1,
3, 6, 12, 20 (food, running)

Library of Congress Cataloging-in-Publication Data
Stevens, Kathryn, 1954–
    Hamsters / by Kathryn Stevens.
        p. cm. — (Pet care for kids)
    Includes index.
    ISBN 978-1-60253-183-3 (library bound : alk. paper)
    1. Hamsters as pets—Juvenile literature. I. Title. II. Series.
    SF459.H3S75 2009
    636.935'6—dc22   2008040001

NOTE TO PARENTS AND EDUCATORS

The Pet Care for Kids series is written for children who want to be part of the pet experience but are too young to be in charge of pets themselves. These books are intended to provide a kid-friendly supplement to more detailed information adults need to know about choosing and caring for different types of pets. They can help youngsters learn how to live happily with the animals in their lives, and, with adults' help and supervision, grow into responsible animal caretakers later on.

CONTENTS

HAMSTERS AS PETS

Hamsters are cute little animals. They are very small and must be handled gently. Hamsters are lots of fun to watch—when they are awake! They sleep for most of the day. They are more active at night.

▸ This girl is holding her hamster gently. Hamsters like this one live for two or three years.

◂ This dwarf hamster is extra small.

GOOD FOOD

Hamsters need foods that keep them healthy. Mostly they eat special hamster food. They also like fresh vegetables, cut up small. A little fruit is good, too. So is a little bit of egg or brown bread. Hamsters need plenty of clean water.

▶ This hamster likes to sit in her food dish while she eats!

◀ Hamster food is a mix of seeds, grains, and other things hamsters like to eat.

A SAFE HOME

A hamster needs a clean, roomy cage. There are many different kinds of cages. Wire ones are good for climbing. Clear tanks, or **aquariums**, also work well. Some plastic cages have fun tunnels and hiding spots. But they can be harder to clean.

▶ Hamsters like to live alone. Two hamsters in the same cage will fight.

◀ Some dwarf hamsters do not mind living together.

A hamster's cage needs **bedding** on the bottom. The bedding should be changed every week. The hamster's bathroom area should be cleaned more often. The cage must have a hanging water bottle. The hamster needs a nest box for sleeping, too.

▶ **Shavings** from aspen trees make great bedding. Hanging bottles like this one keep the hamster's water clean.

◀ Hamsters love to put torn-up paper towels in their nests.

SOMETHING TO DO

Wild hamsters run around a lot looking for food. They also dig and tunnel. Pet hamsters like to do these things, too. They enjoy running on exercise wheels. They love to climb ladders and crawl through tunnels. Pet stores sell toys that are safe for hamsters.

▸ Paper-towel tubes make great hamster tunnels!

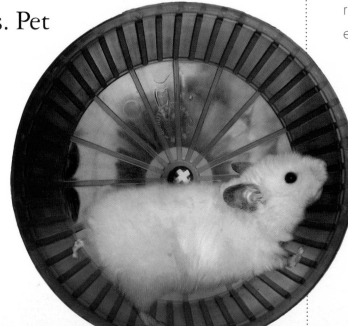

▾ This hamster is running on an exercise wheel.

GOOD HEALTH

Exercise helps keep hamsters healthy. So does good food. Keeping their cages clean is important, too. Sometimes hamsters need to visit an animal doctor, or **vet**. Vets can often help sick hamsters.

▶ A vet is taking care of this sick hamster.

◀ Hamsters can carry germs, so handwashing is important. Very young children should not handle hamsters.

All hamsters need things to chew on. Their teeth grow all the time. Chewing keeps their teeth from getting too long. Hamsters like chewing on wood. Crunchy dog treats are good for chewing, too.

▶ This hamster is chewing on a twig.

◀ Hamsters love to chew on sunflower seeds.

LOVING CARE

Hamsters need people who will take good care of them. Hamsters do not live as long as we might wish. But they are cute and fun. They do not mind being held gently by people they trust. They can make wonderful pets.

▸ These children are playing with their hamster in the evening. They let him sleep during the day.

▾ This hamster feels safe in her owner's hands.

NEEDS:

* a nice big cage
* clean bedding
* a nest box for sleeping
* hamster food
* other healthy foods
* a hanging water bottle
* safe things to chew
* an exercise wheel
* places to tunnel or climb

DANGERS:

* pine or cedar wood
* dogs and cats
* chewing soft plastics
* rough handling
* salty foods, sweets, or chocolate
* getting wet and cold
* strong sunlight

FUR:
Some hamsters have short, smooth fur. Others have long or fluffy fur.

DWARFS:
Many dwarf hamsters are only 3 inches (8 centimeters) long.

SIZE:
Most pet hamsters are about 6 inches (15 centimeters) long.

EARS:
Hamsters have a good sense of hearing.

TAIL:
Hamsters have very short tails.

SLEEP:
Hamsters can get grumpy if you wake them up during the day.

NOSE:
Hamsters have a great sense of smell.

GLOSSARY

aquariums *(uh-KWAYR-ee-ums)* Aquariums are clear tanks where animals can live.

bedding *(BED-ding)* Bedding for hamsters is something they can dig in on the bottom of their cage.

shavings *(SHAY-vingz)* Shavings are very thin pieces cut off of something.

vet *(VET)* A vet is a doctor who takes care of animals. Vet is short for "veterinarian" *(vet-rih-NAYR-ee-un)*.

TO FIND OUT MORE

Books:

Holliman, Peter. *My Hamster and Me*. Hauppauge, NY: Barron's Educational Series, 2001.

Meredith, Susan. *Hamsters*. Tulsa, OK: Educational Development Corporation, 1999.

Rockwell, Ann, and Bernice Lum (illustrator). *My Pet Hamster*. New York: HarperCollins, 2002.

Sabatés, Berta García, Mercè Segarra, Rosa Maria Curto (illustrator), and Sally-Ann Hopwood (translator). *Our New Hamster*. Hauppauge, NY: Barron's Educational Series, 2008.

Video/DVD:

Paws, Claws, Feathers & Fins: A Kid's Guide to Happy, Healthy Pets. Goldhil Learning Series (Video 1993, DVD 2005).

Web Sites:

Visit our Web page for lots of links about pet care:
http://www.childsworld.com/links

Note to parents, teachers, and librarians: We routinely verify our Web links to make sure they are safe, active sites—so encourage your readers to check them out!

INDEX

ABOUT THE AUTHOR

Kathryn Stevens has authored and edited many books for young readers, including books on animals ranging from grizzly bears to fleas. She's a lifelong pet-lover and currently cares for a big, huggable pet-therapy dog named Fudge.

HCOLX   +
        636
        .935
        S

STEVENS, KATHRYN,
HAMSTERS

COLLIER
09/09